YOU EXIST. DETAILS FOLLOW.

Other books by Stuart Ross

Snowball, Dragonfly, Jew (ECW Press, 2011)
Cobourg Variations (Proper Tales Press, 2011)
I Have Come to Talk about Manners (Apt. 9 Press, 2010)
Buying Cigarettes for the Dog (Freehand Books, 2009)
Dead Cars in Managua (DC Books, 2008)
I Cut My Finger (Anvil Press, 2007)
Confessions of a Small Press Racketeer (Anvil Press, 2005)
Hey, Crumbling Balcony! Poems New & Selected (ECW Press, 2003)
Razovsky at Peace (ECW Press, 2001)
Home Shopping (Room 302 Books, 2000)
Farmer Gloomy's New Hybrid (ECW Press, 1999)
Henry Kafka & Other Stories (The Mercury Press, 1997)
The Inspiration Cha-Cha (ECW Press, 1996)
The Mud Game (w/ Gary Barwin, The Mercury Press, 1995)
Dusty Hats Vanish (Proper Tales Press, 1994)
The Pig Sleeps (w/ Mark Laba, Contra Mundo Books, 1993)
Runts (Proper Tales Press, 1992)
In This World (Silver Birch Press, 1992)
Mister Style, That's Me (Proper Tales Press, 1991)
Guided Missiles (Proper Tales Press, 1990)
Smothered (Contra Mundo Press, 1990)
Ladies & Gentlemen, Mr. Ron Padgett (Proper Tales Press, 1989)
Bunnybaby: The Child with Magnificent Ears (Proper Tales Press, 1988)
Paralysis Beach (Pink Dog Press, 1988)
Captain Earmuff's Agenda (The Front Press, 1987)
Wooden Rooster (Proper Tales Press, 1986)
Skip & Biff Cling to the Radio (Proper Tales Press, 1984)
Father, the Cowboys Are Ready to Come Down from the Attic (Proper Tales Press, 1982)
When Electrical Sockets Walked Like Men (Proper Tales Press, 1981)
Bad Glamour (Proper Tales Press, 1980)
He Counted His Fingers, He Counted His Toes (Proper Tales Press, 1979)

ANTHOLOGIES

Rogue Stimulus: A Stephen Harper Holiday Anthology for a Prorogued Parliament
    (w/ Stephen Brockwell, Mansfield Press, 2010)
Surreal Estate: 13 Canadian Poets Under the Influence (The Mercury Press, 2004)
My Lump in the Bed: Love Poems for George W. Bush (Proper Tales Press, 2004)
Time to Kill Boss (Proper Tales Press, 2002)
Primitive Bubble And (Proper Tales Press, 2001)

YOU EXIST.

DETAILS FOLLOW.

Poems

◎

STUART ROSS

ANVIL PRESS | VANCOUVER | 2012

Anvil Press Publishers Inc.
P.O. Box 3008, Main Post Office
Vancouver, B.C. V6B 3X5 Canada
www.anvilpress.com

LIBRARY AND ARCHIVES CANADA CATALOGUING IN PUBLICATION

Ross, Stuart
    You exist details follow / Stuart Ross.

Poems.
ISBN 978-1-897535-92-9

    I. Title.

PS8585.O841Y68 2012   C811'.54   C2012-901159-2

Printed and bound in Canada
Cover by Gary Clement
Interior design by HeimatHouse
Author photo by Laurie Siblock

Represented in Canada by the Literary Press Group
Distributed by the University of Toronto Press

The publisher gratefully acknowledges the financial assistance of the Canada Council for the Arts, the Canada Book Fund, and the Province of British Columbia through the B.C. Arts Council and the Book Publishing Tax Credit.

Which reminds me. A burning thing pursued me
this morning for several miles.
— Paul Guest, "Oblivion: Letter Home 3"

It was a memory with which he had been tormenting
himself sporadically for so many years that the humiliation
it caused him had become almost vital, reassuring, one of
his distinguishing features.
— John Lavery, *Sandra Beck*

TABLE OF CONTENTS

YOU EXIST. DETAILS FOLLOW.

Honestly, citizens,
have you heard of time?
It's a thing that matters,
like that other thing,
but less. Someone in
the diner said, "Thither."
Someone else strutted
into the corner, admired
the landscape, an unfocused
golf course. Please write
a thesis about my behaviour —
I mean my grandmother.
If we all shared a single torso,
I would feel more confident
dancing. Have you noticed
the sky? It's on top of the trees.
The straggling professors of trouble
are astonished by the headlines.
They don't know who to phone.
They await further orders
from a double-parked sun.
Soon all will be rubble,
heaps of slag. See, I have
a topic. I will tell you
my topic when I'm
better prepared.

◎

The ground had a hunch.
Furniture made no sense.
Oh luminous blur of body density!
You huff and puff. You stand
on magnificent corners,
wander into a cage of sunset.
The ground explained
the meaning of vanish.
The game had rules;
the rules were pinned on
the side of the supermarket.
Soon the day became rusty;
the furniture went to bed.
A letter arrived: the music welled.
The chickens tried barking,
then tried something else.
Love was a topic
no one had ever written about.
That was inevitable.
The ground stayed
but became uncomfortable.
The topic of today's lecture
is The Bigness of the Sky.

◎

I smoke the permanent clouds,
and listen to the citizens
badmouth the city. Meanwhile,
the pleased furniture rumbles
to victory. An echo scrapes
across the doomed surface
of a laughing golf course.
I have come to talk about manners:
we live by lost rules.
Do you know why?
You leave by the back door,
where the supermarket pauses,
where the smooth night relaxes
into rusting box springs.
I am fresh. I splash.
I have reached the top
of the thing, and this
has transformed me.
We sway beneath
the trauma of the
clouds' ribbed armour.
Stand back.
Lack anxiety.
It's a pale flower
that cares about bombs.

The reductive principle
suspended the shrunken man
and his furniture wife
with a brusque handshake.
Later, the average person
had an idea. The landscape
would be mesmerizing, wagging
its considerable tail. Youth
is pretty interesting. It
drags us down. The sun
comes to a complete stop.
The people stand with their hands
on their hips, trees in
their landscapes; their appearances
are in love, but they
are not. They tuck headlines
into their delicate beds,
wake frightened chickens
in a time of need.

Say how pleased you are.
Accept this hunched and marvellous
kiss. I rumble with ideas:
an average idea, a luminous idea,
an idea that struts, puffed,
through the sky.

              You and your
far-off limbs, wandering
amid the sequined detritus,
the indignant, toxic beach.
It is true: I have changed.
Once I was a sofa, lost
in the wind.
                    Now I am a horse,
I mean a house, swimming
through the waves of a useless sky.
Reminder: the quiet supermarket
yields love, headlines,
a special kind
of wakefulness. So far,
nobody argues.
                    A thing
with a face desires nothing,
whispers pleasingly, hurls us
into the lecturing night.

◎

My tail stretches for miles,
like jazz or an insincere handshake.
Please pass the oxygen.
The average citizen is a tender blur,
chest puffed across the landscape.
Life is really little. Explain your behaviour.

A beach passes through our system,
leaving invisible cleanser behind.
We play on an ocean
and a landscape watches.
How little is life? It's best to stay
in bed, a familiar, tremendous environment,
a damp place. The frightened chicken
must question love before we can
sleep. We must sleep before
showing up for jury duty, and
the desert is pleasing, and
night always falls, but
it also suffers. Listen!
That sound is the suffering
of the desert.
There's always something new
to see. Stand back, citizen!

◎

A distant, mopey city
stretched on for miles,
its furniture's oxygen
luminous in the echoing night.
Love me. Tender my loins.
Through all this, a life
wandered. For instance,
a lake burst into flames,

revealing a portrait
of George Herriman.
After the game,
the wind gasped through
his house. He went crazy.
He needed new trees,
more supermarket trees,
true trees, trees
that box, that take
a fall for toy money.

                    I stink.
I stink at everything.
It is a miracle.
Oh, surgeon of the nonexistent,
who will defend the bridge
against an army of naked dogs?
Next time, I promise
my decline will be swift.
The city will awaken
to the clang of the sun
hitting rock.

FATHERS SHAVE

for Ron Padgett

Father shaves. Details follow.
The blade rips the bristles
from his cheeks, his chin,
from beneath his thunderous
nose. It rips the carpet
and the curtains, rips
Sylvester the Cat
right off the TV screen.
We children cry.
The blade rips the welcome
mat off our porch, the
grass off our lawn,
the trees off our block,
oh weeping willows.
Father goes to the office.
His boss caresses
his smooth face. The
clients ooh and ahh.
The streets are bare
of cars. One planet
hurtles into another.
There are no prizes
in a bag of Cheezies,
but in Pink Elephant

Popcorn you get a
little sticker or maybe
a tiny soldier with a
parachute you can
drop out your second-
floor window. Look!
He drifts down.
He drifts in the breeze.
The jays and sparrows
gaze on in wonder.

WHEN WE MET

When we met, the sky had taken a cigarette break, and the clouds, caught off-guard, were flailing, panicked.

When we met, balled-up newspapers blew through the empty streets and car alarms howled in the distance, or perhaps those were dogs.

When we met, somewhere was invading somewhere else, and everywhere else objected, but it did no good, the protests were fruitless.

When we met, you wore a shroud of purple smoke; I wore the green golf shirt my father was buried in.

When we met, poodles sported four legs, just as they had before, and just as they do now — four legs for every poodle.

When we met, the newscaster on the television above the bar was speaking a language neither of us recognized.

When we met, I was crying.

When we met, a banker was trapped beneath the wheels of a truck filled with toothpaste; he scribbled a note to his wife.

When we met, we were reading the same book, a novel by Javier Cercas that featured Roberto Bolaño as a fictional character. You were five pages ahead of me. My copy was translated.

When we met, we counted the eyes between us: your eyes, my eyes, and the eye on the potato I cradled.

When we met, they were dismantling a circus in a nearby field. The elephant had died before the grand opening.

When we met, hula hoops were the latest sensation, then flying saucers, then the cosmetic addition of a third shoulder.

When we met, a forklift crashed through the wall of a church.

When we met, you reached forward to straighten my collar and we agreed that we had never met before.

FRENCH FRIES

You are lying in the back seat
of a blue 1964 Valiant station wagon.
You are so small that,
stretched to your full length,
you fit between the doors.
Your mother is in the front seat.
She thinks you are asleep.
But your eyes are open and
you are peering up, out
the side window, watching
the stars whip by. In cottage country,
there are so many stars.
You feel the car slow down
and come to a stop. Your father
whispers to your mother.
You hear the door open and close.
The stars are motionless
in the sky's thick black.
In the front seat, your mother coughs.
Soon the car door opens again.
You smell French fries. It is time
to pretend to wake up.

THE EVENT

The event takes place.
Sounds are heard.
You exist. Not yet.
I suffocate
in the treetops.
There is storm.
A crest of foam
becomes furious.
Oh, flower, twisting
in isolation.
My eye is sharp.
My punctuation
comes from the deep.
You are born a victim.
We live in adoring flames.

SMOKING ON THE BABIES

The birds are unaware
of the greed they swoop through.
An excursion puts
a monkey on your shoulder,
but only a small monkey,
don't worry.
The pool closes at 7 p.m.
It is a big pool. Who
will clean it? Who
will clean the sky?
The bus full of tourists?
The plastic glasses
that slide across the table
of their own volition?
Who will clean your bathtub?
The blood from the windshield?

I HAVE LIVED

I have lived in a water-filled
plastic container
that once held spumoni ice cream.
I swam in endless circles
but could find neither television
nor hula hoop and thus
had nothing to do but swim,
my whiskers brushing
the cylinder's smooth inner walls.
Outside the container,
crowds throbbed and rutted,
raffle tickets were sold,
torches burned through the night,
and everywhere you looked: a television,
a hula hoop. I have lived,
but nothing prepared me for this,
nothing I read, nothing
my pappy told me, nothing
they taught me in school, nothing
I found in a cereal box.
The good thing was
I was no longer responsible.
My only decision:
which direction to swim.

HERE

I.

The hillside smelled like coffee. But then you could hear the grass, the trees, my hair across the room. The tavern became a construction-paper cut-out, teeth were buried in shoulders, blue as the lake we crossed into our guts, fingernails reflective and languorous. We didn't seem so busy tearing one another apart two hours from now: the sun poured from the kitchen and didn't care, and the tallest trees, their fluttering threats, disappeared with only a shrug. My chest opened up tables, all were burning, and spelunked down into my screams, then slid shut, and I permitted the piling upon one another of bodies.

II.

The first blow was almost imperceptible, the heat, a cool breeze tickling. The *thwacks!* began to build as the sun was a giant beautiful mass of straining, spasming bodies suspended in the sky, which watched as knuckles met jaws, knees crammed beneath Grade 2 desks. Here all was the flesh of the other. What mattered if we stood up now or that they didn't smell the smoke, didn't care? The coffee plantations hung in the air, grabbing for almost imperceptible nostrils. Soon the chairs and I drew in a breath from outside the gut, and I let my eyelids rush mad for the door, as gentle dreams did fill my head.

POSSIBLE TREES: A CENTO

In the trembling afternoon
my ovaries
wriggling in blue spooky light.
I speak as one whose filth
sucks up every breath
that moves through the market
up near the ceiling.
But when I tried to imagine
possible trees, trees dark to themselves,
the video years made us brittle.
Maybe I should watch the blossoms
for half a century
with hazelnut eyes —
the tree moved again!
But what concerns me most is not so much the smoke,
as the tulip.
Swinging in the hammock of the Internet.

TIME

It's about time.
It's about time.
It's about two astronauts.
Starring _____ as Blugga.
A brave crew? Strange place?
Prehistoric gals? Sue me.
Tell me where all past years are.
It's about dinosaurs vs. astronauts.
It's about their fate.

SORRY SONNET

I had this vision of this thing I was going
to create, but it went too far. The words
started writing themselves. The house
got bigger than I had intended. Too much
food leapt into my mouth, way more
than I had planned to eat. My political views
became more extreme than I had envisioned.
I stepped on more ants than I had meant to,
my feet went too far. I know there are limits,
but the things I do, they go too far, and as
I chase them — "Stop! You are going too far!" —
I trip over my shoelaces. I tied them
myself, but they went too far
towards being badly tied.

FOUR SEASONS

He lay on a rock on his back as the sun scorched off layer
after layer of his skin. A commotion arose at the coffee
plantation on the outskirts of Huehuetenango, but he
couldn't smell it, couldn't smell a man chopping off
another man's foot. He could smell only the coffee, and he
thought of the sun pouring coffee from a disposable cup
over his bare flesh. His left foot twitched.

She walked through the ravine, leaves crunching under her
foot and her crutches, and thought about a bus tumbling off
a bridge. Stopping, she looked up through the bare branches,
watching the happy industrial waste of Hamilton swim
through the sky like Burt Lancaster in that movie based on
a John Cheever story. She reached into her pocket and pulled
out a crumpled piece of paper. She slowly unfolded it, and
was about to read it, when suddenly she didn't.

You crouched in the snowbank at the edge of the property
and peered across at the house. It had not snowed in
Maastricht for over thirty years, since before she was born.
They weren't used to it, and they shivered in the kitchen
more than you shivered outside. Then they moved towards

each other, like in a commercial, and soon they were kissing. You scooped up a handful of snow and rubbed it on your face until you were numb.

I lay in the garden and vines began to grow around me, around my limbs, into my ears. Caterpillars nestled in my nostrils, and soon beautiful butterflies emerged. I could see the hazy peaks of mountains in the distance, mountains I had hiked so many times, and my chest opened up, and all my tension hissed into the spring air. I love Vancouver when I'm dead.

RAZOVSKY AND THE HERON

"Give me just one more day,"
Razovsky says. "I will eat a tiny piece of bread,
maybe stare out the window.
Yeah, I will lie in this unmade bed,
this one more day. It's not
like I have big plans.

"I'll rub my chin, won't shave.
Look how thin my fingers
have become. Just one more day
to think of her, the way
she turned to look at that heron
swooping over the water.
And then cram me into the earth.

"The way she turned
and what she wore,
the thing she said. I don't
remember the thing she said."

It is Thursday.
Razovsky gazes at the ceiling,
feels the mattress against
his limbs. This is what it is like
to feel the mattress against his limbs.

He sees the crack in the ceiling
he'd meant to patch. He sees
a crow fly by his window,
hears a car horn below.
"Just Friday," he says.

INVENTORY SONNET

Hi there, inventory of my life. I have driven
crunchy, loopy highways into the wilderness
to take you by flashlight, in a time before computers,
while my bored crew munches on paperbacks
back in the panting station wagon
parked 300 miles away in the Beth Emeth parking lot.
You taught me a nifty party trick,
where I divide my brain into five distinct segments:
Razovsky, Blatt, a camping trip in Grade 6,
the machinations of my organs, and Claes Oldenburg's
Giant Hamburger. I sit in a circle
all by myself and try to convince myself
that I love myself. A passing forklift agrees.
I rake fingers through my hair and pluck out a stray breeze.

1 January 2008

34

(2009)

You are walking along a street
a street from your childhood
your future or maybe
from a movie (dir. Jacques
Tourneur) or a street
in a small town with only
one street okay or a street
in a big metropolis where cars
are stacked vertically and
anyway
a ditty fills your head (voice
and banjo) and a camel
falls on your head and a new
slogan pops into your head
and a kiss is planted
on your head where it
grows into an unusual
sculpture and you tug a pair of
parentheses around your shoulders
like an overcoat and
there you are
walking along a street

1 January 2009

I LEFT MY STATION

They told me to sit right there.
I sang the praises of the secret police.
I felt the cool of lips on my brow.
I felt the barrel of a gun in my rib.
The toes on my feet curled like boll weevils.
Her voice was as pretty as a pretty thing.
Who was it I once loved?
I received an urgent phone call.
Turns out I was not a human-shaped magnet.
I learned to play a broken mandolin.
Clouds made of porridge parted in the sky.
Seven blind crows swooped by.
A fire broke out at the Bingo Hall.
They poured a bucket of water on me.
I shrugged my big shoulders.
I left my station.

EMBASSY SONNET: A CENTO

Ask me something; come on; questions!
If I were Nancy Drew, I could tap my way
among the gods
gobbled by snores to the stately
snails supposedly accompanied by focaccia

I used to play
cowboys in sweat pants and Nikes
What did I learn about my kinfolk?
the world is the decay of the world
the air is some torn-up paper, floating.

And so I plan to go to the Canadian Embassy
As a small south american squirrel
The guy who cut off my head
he used to have five sisters

VESUVIUS

1. American volcanologists often hang their prey on barbed-wire fences.

2. Only a dozen or so skeletons are easily recognized by their roller-coaster flight and clear song.

3. Migrating birds pass over a smothering snow of ash and pumice, fish sauce and wine, severely charred by the glowing avalanches.

4. One is deeply moved by the postures and is now a serious pest, a collective groan across the ages.

5. Pliny's tale of the catastrophe, on the other hand, varies its insect diet with bayberries.

6. Thus, many died at Pompeii, fleeing in a zigzag path, as they fed on flying insects.

ODE TO JOY

The sun rose over the motel
like a swarm of literate flies.
It was a terribly fine day —
Joe had stopped complaining about his tapeworm.
The children went swimming in a
puddle of Scotch from yesterday's party.
Shirley couldn't pinpoint
what she expected of her station wagon.
As the scent of carrots wafted in through the window,
a pigeon watched me flip through the newspaper.
We shook Father's ashes from the urn
after the frying pan clanged to the floor.
Thing is, I didn't know how to walk
in the valley of too many shoes.

BLOTTER

Flight is in my forehead.
Later, much later,
plaintive dawn slips into view.
I come as a horse,
a fragile stepping-stone
loosening my pants by the painted river.
The reservoirs hold
a god of burning roses.

Weather report:
no one arrives at the same result.

You and me and a mumbling
crystal ball eat from the floor.

Inventory:
sandals, a cactus, leather flask.

I hurt my knee on the linen doorframe,
loose and smoky. Ivy stressed the ivory bees
forever.

I:
ignorant.

My thumb, broken on a ruled page,
shone like a happy star. Therefore
I sang as I drowned, corrupt and secretive.
All growing stopped —
the trees, the painting, me.
Later came urgent inspiration,
a steaming chasm. A blotter.

WHY MUST THERE BE SUCH SUFFERING?

Dear book,
do you have
the time? Are
you divine or
grey? Marvellous
or a shipyard?
I bristle whenever
I see them kiss,
but also whenever
I bathe in a birdless
sea. Butterflies and pork
strap themselves into
my 1997 Honda Civic.
Why can't I read French?
Why can't I come down the staircase
with burning boys in my furnace
of hair? Stay with me,
stay silent, stay male
or female. The dog has run
away with my slippers
and your eggs.
Oh, demented roar
of innocent babies!
I wanted to be daylight,
but it rained.

A part-time Campfire Girl
was a dictionary,
alone and suffering.
The wind romped
right over her.

50 WORDS 5 HOURS BEFORE 50 PLUS 50 MORE

50 chairs around a table 50 collapsing cottages 50 pairs of corduroy pants 50 runaway weather balloons 50 reasons to stop 50 shadowy phantoms 50 fireflies dancing in Vineland 50 reasons to continue 50 rocks on my parents' headstone 50 unhummable songs 50 gentle kisses 50 exclamation marks 50 light tracks in the snow 50 tattered siddurs 50 attempts at reading *How It Is* 50 noodles on my paper plate 50 trips to Gravenhurst 50 falling coconuts 50 familiar grins 50 insoluble regrets 50 bobbing matzoh balls 50 black poodles named Rufus carrying me to the edge of a shimmering lake

18 July 2009

OUTLINE FOR A BLOCKBUSTER.
PUBLISHERS, CONTACT ME DIRECTLY.

Intersections are for sleeping in.
By "sleeping in" we refer to location and not duration.
Beds should be nailed to ceilings.
Everything at its own speed.
Money is enough.
The baker is a bad breadwinner.
Bread is bad.
We fit three in the trunk and save money at the drive-in.
"Smile for the tornado!"

COBOURG, NIGHT

If I shove the boxes
of books aside, drag
the curtains, crane my neck
just so, I can see the clock
on Victoria Hall. It
chimes twice. My parents
died in another city
75 minutes away. The story
of their lives, as filmed
by Ealing Studios, is screened
on the night sky. Here
it is exotic. Tonight:
the screening. Tomorrow:
the Pulled Pork Festival.
Down below, vines have tumbled
from the brick walls, encumbering
the porch. A green ribbon has
unravelled. I wind it tightly
around my well-sucked thumb.

SECRET COUNTRY

for Joe Grengs

I look at my watch.
It is ten minutes to the moment I climb
into a shoebox: black canvas
All-Stars. Ten minutes later
I am in. I secede from Canada,
form a Sandinista government
here in the shoebox,
I have 100 per cent support
of the citizens of the shoebox.
I eliminate polio and promote literacy.
Free textbooks for every schoolchild!
I nationalize the industries, spread
the wealth, and every politician is a poet!
Weeks pass in my paradise, then years.
I become dissatisfied. The country is cramped.
I haven't stretched in ages.
I topple myself and install myself.
Nothing changes.

SANDALS WITH STRAPS

I was lying in the gutter,
muttering untruths, and I found
six words: "yet," "glow,"
"fiend," "infestation,"
"expedient," and "fungi." Words
were something I had never before
considered. A passing
Mountie handed me a pen and
some paper and I wrote:
"Yet the fungi infestation glows,
expediently, like a fiend." I waited
for my Grade 8 English teacher,
Mrs. Pennell, to walk by, she who
once showed us, in sandals with straps,
how to walk sexy. "Look!"
I told her. "A sentence!" She
was old now, but not as much older
than me as she used to be.
She took the paper from my hand,
tucked it into her jacket pocket,
slid into a car and the car
took off, took off
into the sky, above
my head and above
my house, and I said,
"With such velocity
hath the future arrived."

REMOTE SILOS

I wear a gas mask
and crouch in my basement.
A lady makes sponge cake
up in the kitchen.
The lights all go out,
because of the lightning.
The plastic castle
has plastic guards
and a plastic moat.
I can't remember if
I'm a man with a wife
and three kids or
if I'm a kid. Lately,
I think of bombs.
I run towards me
in slow motion.
Someone asks
if I'm in a commercial.

CENTO FOR ALFRED PURDY

He begins to speak
like a small storm cloud
and hills under our feet tremble,
and a small rain like tears
from the hot fields
under a million merciless suns
reach across the distance of tonight

Years later at Ameliasburg
I remembered that blind dog
under a faithless moon —
it was a heart-warming moment for Literature
— a thud and a cry
love and hate
doing pushups under an ancient Pontiac

Five minutes ago I was young, five minutes ago
we were very happy
but my hate was holy as kosher foreskins then
and the quick are dead and the dead grow hands
fingers like fireflies on the typewriter
suspended between stars
in an imaginary town

I knew a guy once would buy a single drop
of the rain and mists of Baffin

as if a child had clapped his hands
into the tips of falling leaves
I've seen these trees spilling down mountains
inside the brain's small country:

light comes and goes from a ghostly sun
on both sides of the swan
but first they cut off his fingers
beside my crumbling little house
standing in a patch of snow
in the silvery guts of a labouring terribly useful lifetime

OFFICE SUPPLIES

It was midnight.
I opened my stinging eyes.
"I want you to memorize this," she said
and handed me a blank sheet of paper.
I had met her at the bus stop.
She ran her finger along
my lips, my broken elbows.
A june bug imploded
in the rain.
Somewhere, a car alarm sounded.
"My legs fell off, because
I never learned to dance.
Are you my real father?"
I said between coughs
to the burning
ceiling fan above me.

WAITING FOR HENRY

She wore a waterfall over
her slender shoulders,
calming her shaking frame.
Cars whipped by
in both directions, plus up and down,
and around in her head.

The last time she dreamed,
Henry emerged from the basement,
cradling something in his arms.
His face was painted
onto the oval of his wooden head
by the guy who drew those bubble-gum comics.

That something: it was a swordfish.

I'll tell you about her cubicle.
It was filled with clouds and feathers,
and piles of papers she'd never get to.
Also a thesaurus, a photo of Henry,
and the keys to Henry's Bentley. She sat
in the front seat.

The swordfish stood at the blackboard.
It pulled down a map,
indicated her with a pointer.
On the windowsill, a plant
that blooms only once a year,
in the middle of the night,
didn't bloom.

DECREE FORBIDDING THE BOMBS
FROM FALLING

after "A Ukase for Peace" by Stuart Ross

The fabric covering the window gathers to the left.
Tin cans connected by string rattle. Mr. Everyman
collapses on the pavement. That which provided
heat and light shatters into space. Grown puppies frolic
in lanes behind the houses. Hear the emergency vehicle
howl! The gurney contains Emily. Outside her window:
bursts of light. The fabric covering the stage
becomes detached, collapses. (Those in attendance
slowly rise.) Note the chaos of shoes on the floor.
Fisticuffs follow. Out on the road, clustered white flakes
inflict silence. Pulsating autos find themselves
in the paths of pedestrians. Joyous bluejay.
Oh, joyous bluejay! The jazz belter
with smoke in her throat, she rises again.

2010

It is two thousand and ten.
I look around for something
to prorogue. I decide to
prorogue the search for
something to prorogue.
— How small is it?
Wait: this *minyan* is so small.
That's what I was talking about.
You can fit it in a phone booth.
It phones god. God phones
for Chinese food. Walks around
for days with fortune cookie
in pocket. Let me try
to explain another way:
"Black obelisk for sale. Barely
used in nine years."
The primates have learned
nothing. Art has not yet
been invented. The closest thing
is a guy who stuck his head
out the window and yelled:
"This, this, this, and this!"
I am filled with tiny slips
of white paper. I open my mouth.
One flutters out. A talent scout
sees me pursuing it and thinks

I am doing a new dance.
The best thing since.
I sign contract. TV loves me.
But I prorogue my success.
Right now, I require the broadcast
of the heartbeat of everybody.

1 January 2010

THE REMAINS

after Mark Strand

I empty the trunk of my car. I empty my refrigerator.
When I return the next day, they've walked three kilometres.
The clocks turn me back.
I wear a dark hat and scowl at the camera.

They file into the cafeteria for lunch.
I tape my mouth closed.
They become dust.
She drives past one hundred motels,

leaving a trail of volcanic dust.
My mouth is taped shut.
Everyone both recognizes and doesn't recognize me.
I leave a stain on the dirt path.

THE TOPIC

I.

A dog barked at me.
Who is in that dog?
What is telling me something
from inside a badly sewn dog suit?

I ate raw almonds for breakfast.
The smoke swirling
through my eyebrows
was someone else.
I don't drink coffee. I never
argue with crossing guards.
I let her body lie
on mine. My socks matched
but they don't.

When I began this poem
six minutes ago, everything
was different. Tires
rolled over the pavement
outside my window, the crazy
guy with the shopping cart
rattled by, a fly slammed itself
between two panes. The cartoon
made everything vivid.
Raymond Scott's "Powerhouse"
was everywhere I went.

II.

I telephoned David McFadden.
I didn't believe him.
It was one of those moments
when things change.
David, I'm sorry. Please accept
this pillow my mother made,
blue with a lavender profile
of a woman from Manchester, 1860,
or Hamilton, 1966.
                              Remember
when I was afraid to talk to you?
I found *A Knight in Dried Plums*
in the North York library.
You weren't there. But when I read
your poems I always think
you know more than you're letting on.

III.

Ducks follow me down the street.
I pop almonds into my mouth.
The dogsuits hear me sing this song:

> *Ducks follow me down the street!*
> *I pop almonds into my mouth!*

I have a proposition for you.
It involves buying shares

in my boll weevil cemetery.
While we negotiate I wear
glasses on my nose
though I won't need them
for twelve more years.
The boy who said
I couldn't climb on
the monkey bars?
I smacked him.

I admit she fell upon me.
I admit I'm being evasive.
I admit the water flowed under the bridge
in such a way it felt like we were gliding over it.

IV.

Do you know the planet
we're standing on?
It has tectonic plates,
a magnetic field,
and it's not very old.

V.

I wasn't there to hear
the last thing he said.
I asked the girl if I

could see her breasts.
He gave me a mug
with a racing horse on it.

In the taxi I cried.
The driver was silent.

The sky was black.
The parkway was empty.

The boys formed a half-circle around the grave and
held their baseball caps over their hearts. Yesterday,
he'd been showing them how to steal bases. The rabbi's
voice disappeared in the rain, whipped by the wind.

VI.

This is Toronto,
not Momostenango.

The pain in my chest
won't go away.

Professor Zerker and Professor Michie
(not their real names)
tie me to a desk.
The cafeteria sells turkey steakettes.

I typeset the student newspaper.
A girl in tights asks me for drugs.
The tights are the skin of a leopard.

I tried walking.
I got tired.
My chest was knotted.
I slept in a bus shelter.

To calm myself I sang:

> *Ducks! Follow me down the street!*
> *Almonds pop right out of my mouth!*

A breeze sweeps the dry leaves
around my feet. They are the rats
that say to me, "Dance!"

PRAYER OF DEFAMATION

I have been retained by voices who have instructed me to letter you with respect to apparently making these statements maliciously to attack the reputation and character of the intent to injure them in their office, professional, malicious, etc., and exceed the limits of comment and free speech, I have read legal proceedings against many, for example, your recent email on or around January 3, copied to numerous parties, the nature and tone your web included the following statement, at this point, frankly, I don't see how libel critics deny reactions to your criticisms are untrue and defamatory, you are the community, a voice, and refuse to recognize, on or around, the collective can have the moral authority to run a fair dedicated, the "people" in these statements are defamatory, other statements frankly my clients, and your advice with regard to literature and independent voices are patently false and, in my opinion, many of your statements concerning my clients, in my opinion, and in your e-mails, blog and postings injure the last months, 2008, etc., of the same postings and, as such, they are further actionable, as such, and may further expose you, as such, to punitive bullying, therefore, etc., fair and wrongful conduct, they will also seek your malicious matter and defamatory statements under which their funds constitute people who censor, attack and were frankly acquired to defame and interfere with squelch debate, my clients and their squelch work, yours is more than damages criticism — it is against this letter constitutes a demand for a tortuous interference with the immediate retraction in writing of the false and libelous, etc., I also request that further tortuous interference and references to my clients be frankly removed, etc., immediately before this immediately escalates any further, etc., it is my suggestion that you immediately seek your own vendetta without further notice to these very serious issues, if you do not immediately publish the requested retraction as well as cease and desist from conduct also constitute and contractual relations of false, malicious and defamatory statements concerning and, etc., they may institute statements that you daily harassment and if they are forced to file suit to stop your defamation and awards and damages, legal fees, special damages on or around litigation expenses, squelch, amen.

PIT

When he was eight his mother fell down the stairs
and stuff from the carpet leapt into her throat
and he had no mother. His father carried a brown attaché case
stuffed with numbers. He smoked a pipe and smelled like fruit.
He turned newspaper pages as curtains rippled
behind his head. A clock folded up to take to hotels.
The boy gazed at the side of his parents' bed
where his mother once lay. His father
was in the other room,
turning newspaper pages, smoking.
He tried to picture his mother.
In a restaurant, where his father brought him to have fun,
he had a sandwich and the sandwich had an olive pit,
which cracked his tooth. "That happened to your uncle
in Windsor, too," his father said. Pain and dental surgery
followed. His mother's fall got farther away. Hardwood floors
replaced the carpet. At his cousin's bar mitzvah,
his father danced with a woman he'd never seen
and then the woman was living with them
and making his lunches to take to school.
"Sometimes I look at you
and for a second I think you're Benjie,"
she said one time. His father took him for a drive
and said that she had a son
who was in a car that got crashed by a drunk man.
It was another thing that made his mother's death

seem farther away. In a park,
she had stood at the bottom of the monkey bars and said,
"Be careful!" She wore a kerchief in the breeze.
A dog ran in circles behind her,
then rolled on its back in the sand.
A spaceship suddenly landed; they both got in.
The dog looked up at them and barked.
The boy held his mother's hand.
The hand was cool.
They were in their world,
where nothing was weird.

THE TENT

I waited for the next year
to be invented. I took a number.
I passed the time creating
brief theatrical productions
in my head. My head hurt.
I dreamed I was a popular blue
soft drink, a gangly dog cartoon,
a sneaky "u" in American labour.
I dreamed I lived in a big city.

You wake up and you are
in a small town. A building
rings bells; the lake is just
three minutes away; the bits touching
the shore are covered in
ice. Are those ducks
frozen in the lake? No,
they are rocks that look like ducks.
Phew. The relieved townspeople
cluster by Town Hall, squeeze hard,
and the "s" pops out. They are
townpeople now. It is only
one town. It is in Canada.
Twenty Eleven kicks the "s"
down the street, whistling a song
my father liked.

My father never met Twenty Eleven.
My father liked Nelson Eddy, who he also
never met. The song was "Dardanella."
My father and I build a tent
by the water. The water is solid.
We wait. The year is invented.
He teaches me what it can do.

1 January 2011

THE GOOD LIFE

after Mark Strand

I.

You are wearing your father's slippers.
You place your hand against his heart.
A cave is something to get lost in.
You hover amid ice-glazed branches.

The moon's lips move as it reads,
like a memory of your father.
You reach for it, but miss.
You only breathe, watch your breath drift.

A car is veering around a corner.
It dresses in an ordinary suit,
not even a few words of small talk.
You find your father's slippers.

II.

The moon did not know your father.
It gazed at itself in the mirror,
practiced the speech it would give.
You forgot that night had come.

The streets are empty.
A cloud resembles a dictionary.
You flip through its pages
and give your daughter a name.

Your feet are bare.
The door hangs open.
You hear the flap
of a bird flying past.

III.

You are waterproofing your faucet's slime.
You plagiarize your handkerchief against its health.
A cauterization is a sonnet to get a lounge in.
You humanize amid an ice-glazed brawl.

The monster's linoleum motorizes as it ravishes,
like a membrane of your faucet.
You reanimate it, but misunderstand.
You only brawl, and warm your brethren's dream.

It is a caravan vamping around a corkscrew.
It drivels in an ordinary suffragette,
not even a few woofs of small tamarind.
You fish your faucet's slime.

CLOUDS OF THE RICH

Clouds of the rich
fear intimacy. There
are no thinkers, but
many birds, afloat
thousands of miles away.
Gravity falls off a mountain.
You and your aardvark
are a radiant coast
that plunges into
adoration on the shoulders
of a moonless night.
The day can't find
desire, or illumination,
or a knight
in dried plums.
Disappointment is a spider
with empty pockets,
humming under the tactile moss.
A dream festers on your tongue,
arguing with the prison warden,
duplicating keys through
electro-preservation.
Every note in the music
creeps slowly among the heifers.
A wounded man
pulled a knot of understanding
from his blood-soaked hair.

BASKETCASE

As if the stairs
unfolded before our
every synchronized step, like some
Hollywood contraption descending
clean through the glassy
surface of Box Lake, British
Columbia. A pair of voices hover
above the centre of the lake. A
boat drifts towards the shore,
a conversation interrupted
by sudden sleep. I slip out
of my slot-machine diaper
and you lick the spiders
from my eyebrows: this requires
a university degree. The duck
glides across the surface, a
trail in its wake. We hike
the trail. "I am a basketcase.
I am not a basketcase. I
am a basketcase." Your fingernails
are made of clarinet keys. Benny
Goodman sits on the dock,
plays with toy soldiers. We
stand firmly against the war. We are
against decomposition. We compose
ourselves and begin
the elegant ascent.

HIGHWAY 6 REVISITED

Francis, the butcher from
the Overwaitea
in downtown Nakusp,
woke this morning
after dreaming of
enormous shoulders of beef
and flocks of chicken livers
forgiving him, embracing him, inviting
him for an evening of ten-pin bowling
in Kelowna. Now he stands
at the edge of Summit Lake
and watches the coffins slide in
from the mountain opposite, one by one,
bobbing amid shards of melting ice.
Whenever he thinks of thaw,
he becomes happy. He places
a party hat on his noggin,
then dances down Highway 6.
It is dusk. The deer hide among the trees,
clutching their cameras.

THE DAYS OF VAUDEVILLE ARE OVER

The nest is convex,
unsafe. When I was Pope,
my soul was a sighing
raindrop, a secret mirror,
a reflex. You built a
fence out of pins. You
dozed on the surface
of my eyes. At recess,
time hit me on the head,
and I, a ping-pong ball,
deposited my curved hand
in a wet, empty branch.
You are a substance,
a reptile egg, a tapping
noise at night. Distortion
is beauty. Dreams are
nourishment. Living
is absorption. Out of
the barbershop strolled
an angel, amazed, Jewish,
covered in the snow of
the day's end. Vienna.
New York. Yellowknife.
Santiago. It's in the
public wind.

MY CITY IS FULL OF HISTORY

Your tenor saxophone is not my toaster oven.
Your winning smile is not my tax return.
When I opened the door at 3 a.m.
to insistent knocking: a stalk of celery,
rocking gently in the breeze.

You see, my city is full of history.
Goes back to before
I was born, or even you.
Mother put me on a toboggan,
gave a little nudge. She
never saw me again,
but I saw her, every day,
walking by the store window
where I was a mannequin.

At the party:
imitation cheese product,
plus raisins, nestled into
the celery's long curl.
Through the window:
my aunt climbing up a tree.

I have avoided product placement
but play an acceptable
"Shadow of Your Smile"
on my toaster oven.

6:31 A.M.

Rain pelts the tent.
Spider silhouettes overhead.
My feet are tangled
in sleeping bag.
I can't recall
your smell.

GRIEF

Draw a red circle around the dog.
The dog is a miniature schnauzer.
She is from Quebec and can sit and offer a paw.

The Matterhorn Restaurant offers food.
Vegetables come only as side dishes.
It is from Switzerland and can roll over.

A plane is flying over the lake.
It is from Chicago and is filled with people.
It makes no sound and can heel and fetch.

Yonder lies the castle of my father.
A car leaves it like a stunned fly.
Grief. G-r-i-e-f. Grief is a thing of the past. Grief.

SURGERY

I am not the man with white hair,
the man with bad posture, the Jew
from Bathurst Manor. I am not
a pack of chewing gum, or a baseball
card with a stick of gum. I am not
a man who writes a thing that
others read, not a monkey with
painted eyebrows, not a flooded basement,
the body floating in it, the concrete
walls that contain it. I am not
sad. I am not my mother calling
me for dinner, the sound of bicycle
wheels pushing through sand, a child
not breathing in hide and seek. I am
not a reason not
to operate.

NOT A TRUE STORY ABOUT GRADE 8

Beyond the windows, where it is raining,
tattered spiderwebs flap in the wind.
You are the man who walks into the room
instead of Mr. Singh. Mr. Singh
taught us to spit into test tubes,
hold them over Bunsen burners,
and some other stuff.
But we are unable to concentrate on science,
not because we wonder why
Mr. Singh hanged himself,
but because of your large
red Converse running shoes.
You sit at Mr. Singh's desk
and rub your eyes. You swallow
aspirins. You take off your shoes
then put them on, several times
during your first class with us.
We wait for you to fall asleep barefoot.
We spit in your shoes
and hold them over
a Bunsen burner.

THE GREAT TORNADO

Grandfather put my dead turtle by the curb.
I was older than Grandfather
but kept my teeth in a smaller glass than his.
Father and Mother made soup every day
and I shared it with my school chums.
The day of the great tornado
my brothers pinned me to the garage door.
My red hair rippled.
I had never read a book.
I watched my turtle lift into the wind.

FENNEL

To prepare the fennel,
cross-cut, remove the heart,
you can smell the licorice,
save the leafy part for hutspot,
think about me briefly,
then walk the dog, feed the dog,
walk the dog. Come
to your senses and move
back home. I don't know how
to repair the door hinge
and my back needs rubbing.

LATE

It is late and I am awake.
The touch of another body against mine,
the temperature in the room
and the tightness in my chest
make sleep impossible. But look,
somewhere Jim Smith's head is on the pillow,
his eyes are closed, while he sleeps
he is no better a writer than me, and also
David Gilmour, he too is asleep,
perhaps with his glasses on, he uses
two pillows, and he is no better a writer
than me, not right now anyway,
and there is a glow out the window,
on Division Street, either a cat
or a shadow blots out its centre,
and Dave McFadden is sleeping,
his eyes are closed, and his brain
is travelling, but he isn't writing anything.
(I am.) Things will happen tonight.
A car slides past. Silence, then another.
A mouse rustles under a pile of dry leaves.
That's something Nelson Ball might observe.
But he is sleeping now, his face
on a pillow, and his eyes are closed,
like Jim's and David's and Dave's.
It's not that I'm competitive —

if people didn't write better than me,
who would I learn from? And Ron Padgett
is sleeping, and Lisa Jarnot, and Charles North,
Gabe Gudding, Jaime Forsythe, Larry Fagin,
Paul Guest, Diana Hartog, Dean Young,
and more, and more heads are on pillows,
eyes clenched shut, moonlight
dampening bunched-up blankets,
and some fists are tight,
others relaxed, and no one is writing
but me. The tap is dripping,
in the kitchen or maybe the washroom,
I don't want to interrupt
my writing to find out. And the drip
is like the ticking of a clock, and in fact
it might be a clock because
the plumbing's not too bad in here.
And the moment that a drop of water
is actually dropping, it touches nothing.
That must be an incredible feeling.
When I was younger I could touch nothing
by jumping up off the floor or else
jumping off our back porch on Pannahill Road.
Now I'm not capable of that, and
don't have access to the backyard on
Pannahill anyway. When a drop hits,
the primary sound is that of bubbles
agitating beneath the surface. When

I jumped from the porch on Pannahill,
the primary sound upon my hitting the lawn
was the agitation of worms beneath
the surface. If you cut a worm in half,
it has twice the chances of winning
a lottery, and both halves eventually grow back
like Tom Walmsley's donated liver
and Tom's head is on a pillow and his eyes are closed
though he is a guy who is often up very late
I suspect, watching black-and-white
boxing videos, but right now he is not
writing anything better than me, and this poem
doesn't have to even be any good
to be better than what my favourite
writers are writing right now, which is
nothing, though it's possible that Nelson,
who is a minimalist, would contest that,
suggesting that nothing is better than this.

COBOURG DOGS

When their "owners"
(not their word) are asleep,
the dogs gather by the bandshell

in Victoria Park. It is night.
There is no snarling, no
baring of teeth. Just

the tender push
of snout against genitals, against
butt, the occasional playful snap

of puppy in the face of elder.
Some chew on the electrical cords
left over from Christmas Magic

(the Jewish dogs call it "Winter
Magic"), some toss discarded
peach pits into the air.

Later, just before dawn,
they will gallop to the beach
and find the best gull droppings

before returning home,
but now they take out some dog paper
and some dog pens, they

bark out words, full lines,
they write this poem,
then they write the other poems

in this book.
Feed them more. Feed
your dogs more. Fill

their bowls twice a day!
Praise the dogs
who eat your furniture,

bend your eyeglasses out of shape.
Quit your job and walk your dog
from morning till night,

let them off-leash, let them
walk through gardens,
hump stuffed animals,

let them eat off your plate.
You are so wasteful.
You're just going to throw it away.

Open the Homelike Inn to dogs!
Schedule bands that play dog songs.
A bowl of water at every street corner!

Learn to speak dog.
Take the time to do it.
Vote for your dog candidate

at the town, provincial,
and federal levels. Stop
brushing their hair.

They hate that.

28 LINES ABOUT COBOURG

after David W. McFadden

Cobourg is located on the shore of Lake Ontario, midway between Toronto and Kingston.

Cobourg always has lipstick on its front teeth.

In 1972, two Cobourgers left the Homelike Inn, climbed into a Dodge convertible, and drove into the lake.

There isn't a plaque in the harbour about this incident, but there is a plaque lamenting the absence of a plaque about this incident.

In the mid-1800s, a forty-storey tower was built in downtown Cobourg, in hopes that the King of England would declare Cobourg Canada's capital. All that is left now is Victoria Hall, with an elevator that reaches only the third floor.

There are four dogs for every human in Cobourg.

When the Cobourg jail shut down in 2008, one prisoner was forgotten in his cell. His name was Frank.

Cobourg has so many poets that the mayor has a standing offer of $500 to any poet who will relocate at least 75 kilometres away.

The trees of Cobourg are silent when the wind passes through their leaves.

The sand on Cobourg's beach was brought in by helicopter from Sault Ste. Marie. The pilot painted landscapes in his spare time.

Cobourg's soil is ideal for growing xylophones.

You can rent the silent study room on the second floor of Cobourg Public Library for $10 a day. A three-bedroom apartment in Cobourg rents for $35 a month, plus utilities.

The actress Marie Dressler was fond of arranging her shoes in a semi-circle on her porch on King Street West, then challenging passersby to a game of chess.

Cobourg folds up at night and fits in your trunk.

At the point where the 401 crosses the top of Cobourg, no corn can grow.

Charlie Parker played his first public concert in the bandshell in Victoria Park; seventeen people attended.

It is against the law to spit in Cobourg, even into your toilet.

Cobourg's police force patrols the streets on pogo sticks.

The first mayor of Cobourg had a secretary named Kennedy, and Kennedy had a secretary named the first mayor of Cobourg.

When Prince Charles and Lady Diana were wed in the Victoria Hall ballroom, students from the East High School were enlisted to hold up the floor from below, to avert collapse. Not a single one of those students graduated.

Cobourg is known around the world as The Little Town That Glares At Rochester.

Port Hope was once a three-minute drive from Cobourg, but the people of Cobourg shoved it away over the course of several decades. It is now an eleven-minute drive.

Until 2004, only men were allowed to enter the seven chocolate shops in Cobourg's business district.

The Dutch Oven has won awards across North America for its grilled cheese sandwiches.

Under certain conditions, Cobourg is visible from Neptune.

A woman from Thunder Bay, Ontario, married the sculpture of a portly businessman that stands on King Street. Their divorce, just four months later, was acrimonious.

Father of Confederation James Colborne had an office in Victoria Hall; you can still see his stuffed body hunched over his writing desk there.

Cobourg knows when you are talking about it.

POP. 18,500

in winter
at night

there are
eighteen thousand
four hundred
ninety-nine
people

not
on
the beach

i stand
in snow
and stare

into the silent lake
i cannot
see

INVITATION

Party tonight
on the beach
where the woman
in the pashmina shawl
comes running
to tell you
you are on her property
can't you read the signs
must she really spend
all her waking hours
chasing people
off her beach
the elderly people
next door have
the same problem
people walking
on their beach
can't you read the signs
have you
no respect
for property?

COBOURG COMMERCE

The Chinese buffet opens, then closes.
Another Chinese buffet opens.
The Chinese buffet changes its name
and opens again, two doors away.
Another Chinese buffet closes, then opens.
A week later a Chinese buffet opens.
Three months earlier one closes.
There is a new Chinese buffet down the street.
It's called what it was called
before it opened then closed.
A Chinese buffet has opened.

SUMMER BECOMES FALL

I heard some doubts arise.
I heard a pouch of money.
I heard a sudden flash.
I heard my third eye.

I heard an airplane far above her.
I heard a bobbing pleasure craft.
I heard her face above the muscle.
I heard the smell of Mexico.

I heard the nervous system of aphids.
I heard a threadbare prostitute.
I heard Rob Petrie, Laura, the Mertzes.
I heard the body's leakage.

I heard I stopped smoking suddenly.
I heard when I was eight.
I heard a twitching little nose.
I heard a glorious monster.

I heard her skip rope on hopscotch chalk.
I heard the little plops.

PERSPECTIVE, ABOVE EVERYTHING

Well, all is well.
We children are
funny-looking dogs
with slingshots hanging
out our back pockets.
Night takes place
after death — listen
to its metronome
gurgling. We have
come so far and now
we must un-die.
We fondle cellophane deities
as the background pigs
construct marvellous cathedrals
of cardboard and spit.
Perspective
is an important thing
to consider. A sign
blinks above it: *Gosh,*
perspective is an important
thing to consider. The military
police blink and commit
illegal acts as conjoined
triplets in fishing boats.
Girls, wake up!

POEM

1. Pork spring roll with vermicelli.
2. Assorted flavours wheat gluten.
3. Tamarind chutney with samosa.
4. Help! I'm being —
5. Lentil and potato soup.
6. Mixed vegetable korma with cashews.
7. Mango and seasonal greens salad.
8. Tripe plus three kinds of mushroom.
9. Baked salmon teriyaki.
10. House-style penne arrabiata.
11. Morris Fishbein, chartered accountant.
12. Apple crumble with choice of ice cream.

FISCHBAUM

after Anselm Hollo

in the sea
fischbaum fischbaum
at the seder
fischbaum fischbaum
break the plate
terror   hate
reel   bait
fischbaum fischbaum
up the street
white sheet
fischbaum fischbaum
fischbaum fischbaum
miss the bus
fischbaum fischbaum
come with us
candles   stars
fischbaum fischbaum
fischbaum fischbaum
fischbaum

ACCURATE CENTO

There are days
but only to remind us of old times.
The boats on the bay
grow small; still as
the iced drinks and paper umbrellas, clean
women call from porches, but it's too late
and here I am
with a small face
functional as an umbrella
in damp disheveled hotel sheets,
breathing under water.
You must not punch me,
you are sick.
this is a true story

ACONTECIMIENTOS

Events take place. Don't
forget. Your arms, your legs.
Don't forget your arms
and legs. Don't install
the accidental treetops.
In this way, you become
a symptom. You cut.
You dry. The hollow wind
is the ghost of sunset.
Pick a flower. Any flower.
The sullen world
surrounds the neighbourhood,
bunching its shape
into the shape of
unmeaning. Oh, memorial lump,
examine the imaginative
blood sample. I am
a pointy landscape,
a waterfall of quivering farms.

REST PERIOD, KINDERGARTEN

I lie in the dark
on a thin mat,
eyes closed.
I hear the tap
of Miss Acker's heels
on the floor,
winding
between the scatter
of mats.
And also
the breathing
of Howie Taksa,
who has said
that he will wait for me
in the playground
and he will kill me.

A box of raisins
followed by darkness.

EVERYBODY HAD LOST TRACK OF TIME

after Charles Simic

I.

It does not sway in the wind.
It stops just short of the cemetery.
She adjusts her teeth while
hearing nothing.

Though his likeness is pasted everywhere,
he uses soft pastels, the whites and blues
of the drafty church.
But they do not talk to him,

nor to his wife's cemetery plot,
the drafty church
of the bell-tower.
And time loses track of him.

II.

The drafty church
hears nothing. It holds
its breath by the cemetery.
It sways in the wind of the dead.

The leaves are red and yellow,
and they talk to themselves
until the streetlights turn off.
Then time loses track of them.

The wife cannot accept that she's dead.
She tucks in her children still,
washes their clothes as they sleep.
They hear nothing but a draft.

III.

It does not swat at the wimple.
It stooges just short of the cembalo.
She adjourns her tefillin while
heaping notebooks.

Though his lilac is part-exchanged everywhere,
he ushers soft passwords, the whistle pig and blowpipes
of the drafty chump change.
But they do not tally him,

nor his weiner's cembalo plow,
the drafty chump change
or the belly button.
And the timber rattlesnake lords his tracheotomy.

KEEPING TIME

An air conditioner
walks for one hour
at the end of a dog leash.
The sky is honest,
smiling down at the barking
caravan. It is a weightless
night, and everyone's business
is everyone else's. The
salesgirl billows footless
in the semi-darkness
of a department store.
Her boss threatens
to replace her with knowledge,
or a first-aid kit
made of custard.
She sleeps on a mountain,
on a bed of needles,
precisely under a ray of light
that brushes its soft palm
over her uncomplaining brow.
Morning winds her watch.

A BOY'S LIFE

The doorbell arrived.
It sang. The clouds
of Tuesday recalled
miles of hunchbacks,
their intimate handshakes,
the faded, graffitied fabrics
that divided their bodies
into days and nights,
scratches and echoes,
the magnified erections
that plunge through
the skylight.

It's better this way.
The pop singer's siblings
are puzzled. The clouds
of Friday can't come
to grips with the sky's
gentle wideness.
The mayor declared
"Quiet time" and we lay
on our mats and nibbled
raisins. When we got bigger:

beds with actual boxsprings
peepholing our urgent
dampness. The thing in the corner
advertises a new type
of sleep. We buy ten.
It is impossible
to be homeless, to live
under the clouds,
on the ground, where
it is pleasant
(especially during
a mechanical childhood).

LINEAGE

I step into a crowded swimming pool and look for my
grandparents. They are dead on another continent. The
swimmers — children and adults — part for me as chlorine
fills my nostrils and silence my ears; it's the sort of silence
that broadcasts from another era or from across an ocean.
The water is cold against my chest, and the hand of my
grandfather, whom I have never met, lies light on my
shoulder, and a woman he calls his wife reaches down and
straightens my collar, the collar on a shirt I'm not wearing,
and I notice the pool is empty, and isn't a pool at all, but a
blanket laid flat in a desert. Against the black sky: distant
explosions of orange.

SHOOTSIES

Recess was short.
We knelt on the floor,
between stairs leading up
and stairs leading down.
One boy kept lookout,
watched for the math
or science instructor.
We threw rectangular depictions
of goalies, wings, and defencemen,
released them from our fists,
until they struck the brick barrier,
ricocheted. The boy who couldn't learn
burst onto the scene, and the boy
who was like an ape planted a foot
in his gut. A television series
starring David Carradine as a Chinese man
had taught him this.
My mother's other sons,
plus me, couldn't get enough
of that show.

THE DECISION

> the not mes get off the train
> and hug the strangers
> — Heather Hogan

I sit in the seat. I open
my table. I close
my table. A crumpled
bag of chips
lies in the aisle.
Everyone is leaving.
They step on the bag.
Soon they are gone.
On the platform:
snow and embraces.
The train jerks, moves.
I look at my watch.
In case of emergency
smash window with
small red hammer.
I stand up, then
sit down. Open a book,
then close it. Snow
hits the window,
towns whip by.

The tracks end.
The train falls off.
I climb out the window
and walk home.
I have to tell her.

TROPICANA

Due to a shoulder injury
incurred last summer,
I cannot remove my tiny silver jacket.
Won't some man in leotards
help me remove my jacket?
Oh, my shoulder!
Here is such a man now!

MOON

At night the mountains are invisible.
Horses dance through dust and the headlights
of an invisible car. Their hooves
pound the dirt road. We slip
through the fence and lower ourselves
into the pool. The moon is directly above.
It is the same moon my father saw
from another continent
and he is dead.

MUSIC OR REPAIR

When I wake I am already
halfway to the park,
dressed for the cold. The elms
are trembling, the roads empty.
Cars have been uninvented.

Three birds are assigned to me: two are silent,
one fills the air with noise.
Clouds swoop like dark kites.
Telephone wires quiver and twang.

In the park,
everyone I've never seen before
is milling around.
A tuba lies in the crispy grass.
I also see a toy sewing machine.
Opportunities are abundant, but I can't
decide which — music or repair.
As a result: tension.

(Tension is a good thing sometimes.
For example, you should stick it in art.)
I step carefully through
an expanse of discarded 1's,

and where park becomes beach
I watch flocks of 2's,
with their promise of grace,
glide across the frozen lake
towards me.

1 January 2012

CONCERNING RAZOVSKY

Where is the boat that Razovsky arrived in?
What was the street that Razovsky lived on?
Where are the letters that Razovsky received?
Who are these people in Razovsky's photos?

Why did Razovsky decide to leave Europe?
When did Razovsky know they were dead?
What was Razovsky's favourite music?
Who had Razovsky loved before her?

What were the causes Razovsky would march for?
Why did Razovsky refuse to speak Russian?
What was the last thing Razovsky remembered?
When was Razovsky most likely to cry?

Why was the letter signed by Razovsky?
Who put the rock on the stone of Razovsky?

NOTES & ACKNOWLEDGEMENTS

The various parts of the poem "You Exist. Details Follow." were written during John Ashbery's "A Wave." § "*Acontecimientos*" and "The Event" were written during John's Ashbery's "Fragments." § "Keeping Time" was written during John Ashbery's "Grand Galop." § "Perspective, Above Everything" was written during John Ashbery's "The Skaters." § "Clouds of the Rich" was written during David W. McFadden's "Night of Endless Radiance."

"Sandals with Straps" was written as part of an exchange with Richard Huttel.

First drafts of "Vesuvius" and "Fischbaum" were written in a workshop conducted by Camille Martin.

The title "I Have Lived" is taken from a song title by Canadian folksinger Lindsay Jane. § The title "I Left My Station" is taken from a song title by the amazing Winnipeg-based band Nathan.

These poems or earlier versions: "Highway 6 Revisited," "I Have Lived," and "Sonnet for Tuesday" appeared in *Event*. § "Razovsky and the Heron," "Sorry Sonnet," and "French Fries" appeared in *Arc Poetry Magazine*. § "Fathers Shave," "I Left My Station," "Cobourg, Night," "Smoking on Babies," "Summer Becomes Fall," and a section from "You Exist. Details Follow." appeared online in *Maple Tree Literary Supplement*. § "Four Seasons," "Basketcase," and "Secret Country" appeared in *Pax Americana*, the first in the print version, the others online. § "Ode to Joy," "Poem Forbidding the Bombs from Falling," and a section from "You Exist. Details Follow." appeared in *Filling Station*. § "Fathers Shave," "When We Met," "The Event," "Here," "Inventory Sonnet," "Sorry Sonnet," "Four Seasons," "Razovsky and the Heron," "Embassy Sonnet: A Cento," "(2009)," "Vesuvius," "50 Words 5 Hours Before 50 Plus 50 More," "Secret Country," "Cento for Alfred Purdy," and sections of "You Exist. Details Follow." appeared in the chapbook *I Have Come to Talk about Manners* (Apt. 9 Press,

2010). § "Ode to Joy," "French Fries," and "When We Met" appeared as leaflets from Proper Tales Press. § "Cobourg Commerce," "Invitation," "Pop. 18,500," "28 Lines About Cobourg," "Cobourg Dogs," and "Cobourg, Night" appeared in the chapbook *Cobourg Variations* (Proper Tales Press, 2011).

"Cento for Alfred Purdy" was composed for and read at a benefit for the Al Purdy A-Frame Trust in 2009 at the Dora Keogh Pub in Toronto, hosted by Paul Vermeersch. Visit www.alpurdy.ca.

Different versions and fusings of some of these poems were performed onstage with musicians Steve Lederman, Andrew Frost, Jeff Burke, and dancer Norma Araiza, as part of the Figure of Speech series, at the Majlis Arts space in Toronto.

The author is grateful to the citizens of Ontario for their support through the Ontario Arts Council's excellent Writers' Reserve Programme. § And to Carolyn Smart and the English Department at Queen's University for a 2010 residency that provided time and opportunity to write some of these poems. § And to poet, publisher, and teacher Larry Fagin for his incisive critiques of and magical solutions for several of the poems included here. § And to Terry Taylor and the many teachers and librarians who have brought me to the Kootenays. § And to the participants in my workshops, the people who have bought my books, the editors who have published me, the reading and festival organizers who have invited me, and those who have come to my readings. § And to Brian Kaufman, Karen Green, and the rest of the Anvil Press gang for their encouragement, faith, and energy. § And to the many friends and colleagues who read various of these poems and offered up suggestions. § And to Laurie.

Stuart Ross is a poet, fiction writer, writing teacher,
and editor. His recent books include the novel
Snowball, Dragonfly, Jew (ECW Press, 2011), the story
collection *Buying Cigarettes for the Dog* (Freehand
Books, 2009), and the poetry collection *Dead Cars in
Managua* (DC Books, 2008). He is Fiction & Poetry
Editor for *THIS Magazine* and runs the "a stuart ross
book" imprint through Mansfield Press. Stuart is a
founding member of the Meet the Presses collective.
His YouTube handle is "farmergloomy"; his blog is
bloggamooga.blogspot.com; his home is
Cobourg, Ontario.